Thoreau
at Walden

Thoreau
at Walden

by John Porcellino
from the writings of
Henry David Thoreau

with an introduction by D.B. Johnson

SCHOLASTIC INC.
New York Toronto London Auckland
Sydney New Delhi Hong Kong

Cover design by Michel Vrána.
Production design by James Sturm & Michel Vrána.

ISBN-13: 978-0-545-65629-0
ISBN-10: 0-545-65629-X

1 2 3 4 5 6 7 8 9 10   31   22 21 20 19 18 17 16 15 14 13

Introduction

by D. B. Johnson

After graduating from Harvard at twenty years old, David Henry Thoreau returned home to Concord, Massachusetts. Like many recent graduates, he was forced to ask himself: What am I going to do with my life?

He toyed with the idea of being a minister, a lawyer, a doctor, and a businessman. He decided to teach public school, but that didn't last long—he quit when he was ordered to flog his students. People in Concord thought Thoreau was crazy to throw away a good job just because he was against beating a student; kids had always been whipped in school. Their suspicion that Thoreau was a bit strange was confirmed when he changed

his name to Henry David. They just shook their heads. Who did he think he was to change his christened name like that? Well, Thoreau thought Henry David sounded a lot better than David Henry. And anyway, "Henry" was what his family had always called him.

After his attempt at teaching, he began working at his father's pencil factory. He invented a better pencil, with a harder and blacker lead, that was as good as the finest pencils from Germany. The small John Thoreau and Sons factory grew, but business did not make Thoreau happy. So Thoreau was, once again, left trying to figure out what to do.

At the time, his good friend and

mentor, Ralph Waldo Emerson, was quickly gaining fame as a writer and public speaker. Thoreau aspired to be more like him. On October 22, 1837, he began writing in a journal every day.

The craft did not come easily to Thoreau. He was living in his parents' home, which was noisy with boarders and visiting relatives. But living somewhere else would cost money. He would need a job, and then he'd have no time to write. Just when his life seemed most miserable, his brother became seriously ill. Thoreau nursed him through the final days and was greatly upset by his death. He grew silent and depressed for months, even showing all the symptoms of his brother's illness. When he recovered, he was more determined than ever to get down to writing and making something of himself.

It was three more years before everything fell into place. Emerson bought a woodlot two miles from the village on Walden Pond. Thoreau proposed to build a small cabin there to live in and write full-time. For food, he would plant a garden large enough to feed himself as well as sell some beans and potatoes to buy rice, molasses, flour, and other things he needed. This would be his "experiment in living." By stripping his life bare, he did not need to earn much money. He spent all his time studying and writing when he was not hoeing his seven-mile-long row of beans. Most important, he lived surrounded by nature, and in harmony with it.

He bathed in the pond. Birds flew through his open windows. He went to sleep to the sound of whip-poor-wills and owls. He cooked his meals outdoors in summer. He spent days sitting in the woods or floating on the pond listening to what nature had to say. Others had tried to live this way, but Thoreau was the first to think of it as an experiment that he would record in every detail.

Thoreau was not a hermit. He went to the village often—to visit family and friends, to do odd jobs, and to observe his neighbors at work. On one visit, he was arrested and jailed for not paying his poll tax. As an abolitionist who was against the Mexican-American war, Thoreau objected to giving the government his monetary support, and allowed himself to be arrested rather than pay the tax. Though he spent only one night in jail (someone paid his tax for him), the experience focused his thoughts on what duties a man owed to the state. If the government was unjust, was it his duty to support it anyway? And if he refused to support the government, how should he oppose it? He concluded that it was possible and even necessary to peacefully disobey unjust laws, to go to jail as he had, in order to change the laws or the government. When a government supports an evil like slavery or an unjust war, it is the duty of citizens to resist peacefully, to withhold their support. Thoreau's night in jail led him to write "Civil Disobedience."

It is no surprise that many people in Concord found Thoreau's ideas and his behavior strange. They could not understand why he was wasting his education wandering in the woods. What did he do all day? Others wanted to know how he lived on so little. And why would he choose to live with so few comforts? What did he eat? Why did he live so far from town? How could he be strong if he

"I grew in those seasons like corn in the night, and they were far better than any work of the hands would have been. They were not time subtracted from my life, but so much over and above my usual allowance." —HENRY DAVID THOREAU

ate only vegetables and grain? Wasn't he lonely?

When his experiment was over, Thoreau answered all these questions in several lectures at the Concord Lyceum. He made his case: If you get rid of all but the most necessary things, if you live simply and in harmony with nature, and let your passion be your work, you "will meet with a success unexpected in common hours."

Thoreau's journal entries, from March 1845 to September 1847, would become one of the greatest books in American literature: *Walden; or, Life in the Woods*. It has been translated into dozens of languages and read all over the world. It spurred countries to set aside land for national parks and to preserve natural habitats for everyone's health and enjoyment. Thoreau's great essay, "Civil Disobedience," which also grew out of his experiences during this time, inspired the overthrow of British rule in India and the movement toward civil rights in America.

In this book, John Porcellino has captured the spirit of *Walden*. You may regret that not all of Thoreau's words are here, but I do not. His words are among the most quoted of any writer and are found everywhere today. What could not be found until now are the countless moments of silence that Thoreau experienced at Walden Pond. Porcellino faithfully re-creates those moments of quiet reverie, of Thoreau sitting in a sunny doorway or in the woods, soaking up the passing of time. It seems as if nothing is happening. Then we experience it too, just as Thoreau did when he wrote, "I grew in those seasons like corn in the night, and they were far better than any work of the hands would have been. They were not time subtracted from my life, but so much over and above my usual allowance."

—D. B. J.

Prologue

CONCORD, MASSACHUSETTS - 1845

CONCORD
1 MI.

THE MASS OF MEN LEAD LIVES OF QUIET DESPERATION...

I SEE YOUNG MEN, MY TOWNSMEN, WHOSE MISFORTUNE IT IS TO HAVE INHERITED FARMS, HOUSES, BARNS, CATTLE and FARMING TOOLS...

FOR THESE ARE MORE EASILY ACQUIRED THAN GOT RID OF...

WHY SHOULD THEY BEGIN DIGGING THEIR GRAVES AS SOON AS THEY ARE BORN?

IT IS VERY EVIDENT WHAT MEAN and SNEAKING LIVES MANY OF YOU LIVE...

... ALWAYS ON THE LIMITS...

TRYING TO GET INTO BUSINESS and TRYING TO GET OUT OF DEBT...

MAKING YOURSELVES SICK,
THAT YOU MAY LAY UP
SOMETHING AGAINST A
SICK DAY...

BUT MEN LABOR UNDER A MISTAKE...

...THEY HONESTLY THINK THERE IS NO
CHOICE LEFT.

IT WOULD BE SOME ADVANTAGE TO LIVE A PRIMITIVE and FRONTIER LIFE, THOUGH IN THE MIDST OF AN OUTWARD CIVILIZATION

...IF ONLY TO LEARN WHAT ARE THE GROSS NECESSARIES OF LIFE and WHAT METHODS HAVE BEEN TAKEN TO OBTAIN THEM...

SHALL WE ALWAYS STUDY TO OBTAIN MORE OF THESE THINGS...

and NOT SOMETIMES TO BE CONTENT WITH LESS?

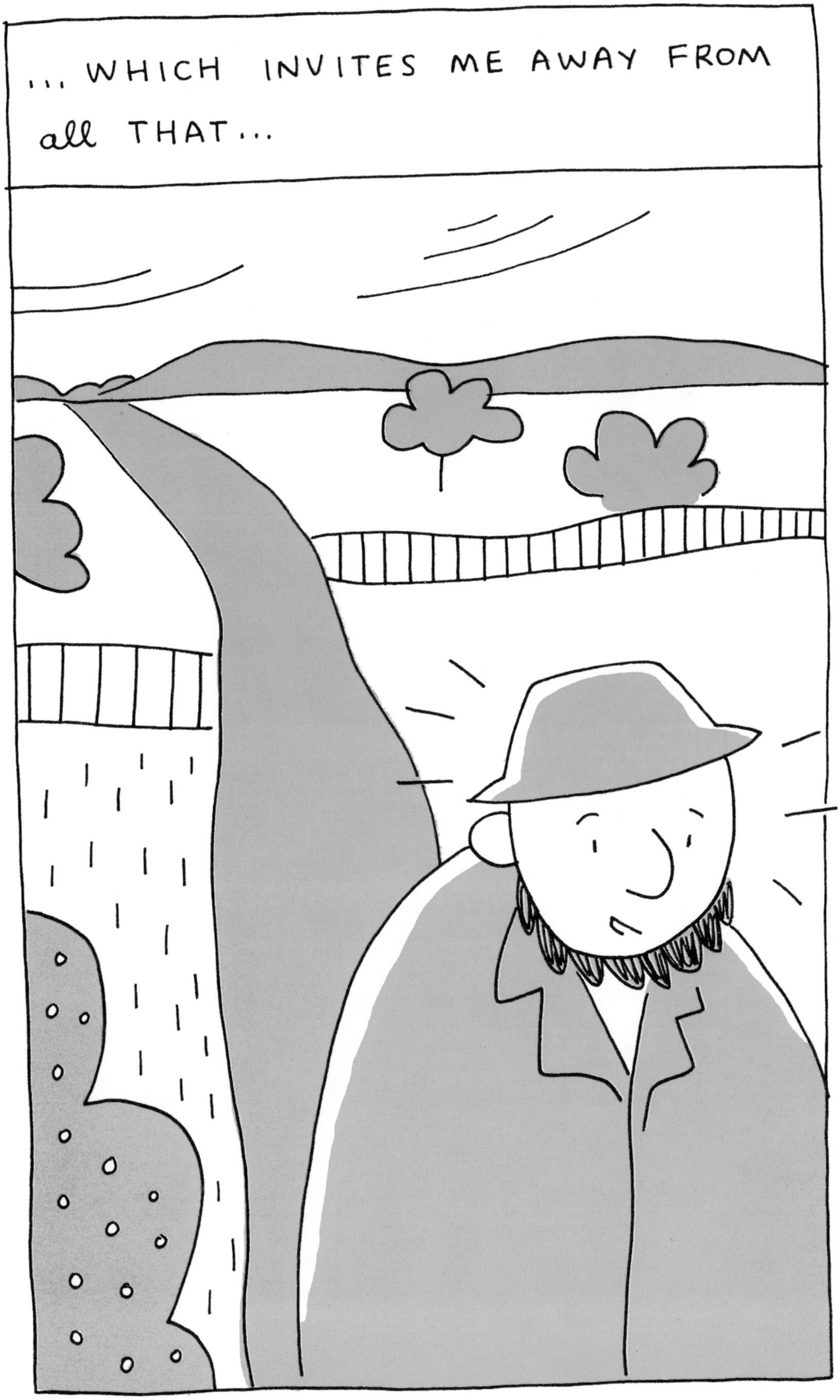
...WHICH INVITES ME AWAY FROM all THAT...

Part One

WALDEN POND
-1846-

and EARNED MY LIVING BY THE LABOR OF MY HANDS ONLY...

TO BE A PHILOSOPHER IS NOT MERELY TO HAVE SUBTLE THOUGHTS, NOR EVEN TO FOUND A SCHOOL, BUT TO SO LOVE WISDOM AS TO LIVE ACCORDING TO ITS DICTATES...

A LIFE OF SIMPLICITY, INDEPENDENCE, MAGNANIMITY, and TRUST.

IT IS TO SOLVE SOME OF THE PROBLEMS
OF LIFE — NOT ONLY THEORETICALLY—

BUT PRACTICALLY...

MY PURPOSE IN GOING TO WALDEN POND WAS NOT TO LIVE CHEAPLY, NOR TO LIVE DEARLY THERE, BUT TO TRANSACT SOME PRIVATE BUSINESS WITH THE FEWEST OBSTACLES...

HOW TO GET MY LIVING HONESTLY, WITH FREEDOM LEFT FOR MY PROPER PURSUITS...

I LONG AGO LOST A HOUND, A BAY HORSE, and A TURTLE-DOVE...

and AM STILL ON THEIR TRAIL.

CRONCH!

HOWEVER MEAN YOUR LIFE IS, MEET IT and LIVE IT...

... I AM CONVINCED, BOTH BY FAITH and EXPERIENCE, THAT TO MAINTAIN ONE'S SELF ON THIS EARTH IS NOT A HARDSHIP BUT A PASTIME, IF WE WILL LIVE SIMPLY and WISELY...

... THERE MAY BE AS MANY DIFFERENT PERSONS IN THE WORLD AS POSSIBLE, BUT I WOULD HAVE EACH ONE BE VERY CAREFUL TO FIND OUT and PURSUE HIS OWN WAY...

IF A MAN DOES NOT KEEP PACE WITH HIS COMPANIONS, PERHAPS IT IS BECAUSE HE HEARS A DIFFERENT DRUMMER...

LET HIM STEP TO THE MUSIC WHICH HE HEARS...

HOWEVER MEASURED OR FAR AWAY.

Part Two

ONE OF THE ATTRACTIONS OF COMING TO THE WOODS TO LIVE WAS THAT I SHOULD HAVE THE LEISURE and THE OPPORTUNITY TO SEE THE SPRING COME IN...

EVERY MORNING WAS A CHEERFUL INVITATION TO MAKE MY LIFE OF EQUAL SIMPLICITY, and MAY I SAY INNOCENCE, WITH NATURE HERSELF.

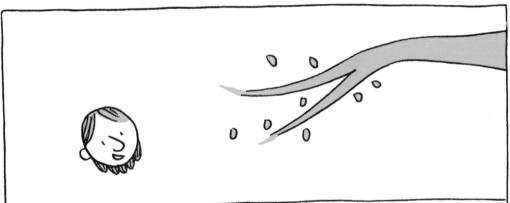

SYMPATHY WITH THE FLUTTERING ALDER and POPLAR LEAVES ALMOST TAKES AWAY my BREATH.

WHEN I FIRST PADDLED ABOUT ON WALDEN, IT WAS COMPLETELY SURROUNDED BY THICK and LOFTY PINE and OAK WOODS...

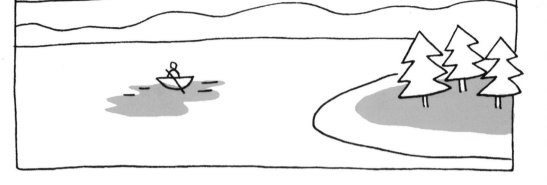

and IN SOME OF ITS COVES GRAPEVINES HAD RUN OVER THE TREES NEXT TO THE WATER

and FORMED BOWERS UNDER WHICH A BOAT COULD PASS...

THE HILLS WHICH FORM ITS SHORES ARE SO STEEP, and THE WOODS ON THEM SO HIGH...

... IT HAD THE APPEARANCE OF AN AMPHITHEATRE FOR SOME KIND OF SYLVAN SPECTACLE...

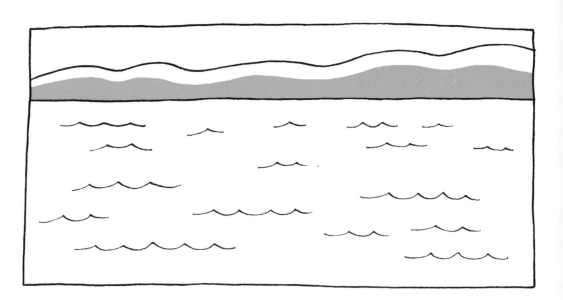

A LAKE IS THE LANDSCAPE'S MOST BEAUTIFUL FEATURE...

IT IS EARTH'S EYE

LOOKING INTO WHICH THE BEHOLDER MEASURES THE DEPTHS OF HIS OWN NATURE.

I PLANTED ABOUT FIVE ACRES and A HALF OF LIGHT and SANDY SOIL... CHIEFLY WITH BEANS, BUT ALSO A SMALL PART WITH POTATOES, CORN, PEAS, and TURNIPS...

I CAME TO LOVE MY ROWS, MY BEANS.

COMMONLY, I RESTED AN HOUR OR TWO IN THE SHADE AT NOON, AFTER PLANTING, and ATE MY LUNCH, and READ A LITTLE BY A SPRING WHICH WAS THE SOURCE OF A SWAMP and OF A BROOK, OOZING FROM UNDER BRISTER'S HILL, HALF A MILE FROM MY FIELD...

THE APPROACH TO THIS WAS THROUGH A SUCCESSION OF DESCENDING GRASSY HOLLOWS, FULL OF YOUNG PITCH PINES, INTO A LARGER WOOD ABOUT THE SWAMP. THERE, IN A VERY SECLUDED SPOT, UNDER A SPREADING WHITE PINE, THERE WAS A GREAT FIRM SWARD TO SIT ON...

YOU ONLY NEED SIT STILL LONG ENOUGH IN SOME ATTRACTIVE SPOT IN THE WOODS THAT ALL ITS INHABITANTS MAY EXHIBIT THEMSELVES TO YOU...

I HAVE, AS IT WERE, MY OWN SUN and MOON and STARS, and A LITTLE WORLD, all TO MYSELF...

SOME OF MY PLEASANTEST HOURS WERE DURING THE LONG RAIN STORMS IN THE SPRING OR FALL...

WHEN AN EARLY TWILIGHT USHERED IN A LONG EVENING IN WHICH MANY THOUGHTS HAD TIME TO TAKE ROOT and UNFOLD THEMSELVES...

BOOM!

"LET THE THUNDER RUMBLE...

TAKE SHELTER UNDER THE CLOUD..."

IN THE MIDST OF A GENTLE RAIN, WHILE THESE THOUGHTS PREVAILED, I WAS SUDDENLY SENSIBLE OF SUCH SWEET and BENEFICENT SOCIETY IN NATURE...

IN THE VERY PATTERING OF THE DROPS... and IN EVERY SOUND and SIGHT AROUND MY HOUSE...

...AN INFINITE and UNACCOUNTABLE FRIENDLINESS all AT ONCE, LIKE AN ATMOSPHERE SUSTAINING ME...

... EVERY LITTLE PINE NEEDLE EXPANDED and SWELLED WITH SYMPATHY...

...and BEFRIENDED ME...

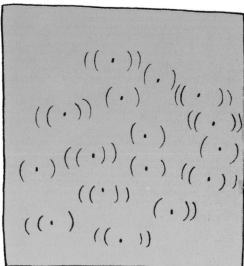

A SINGLE GENTLE RAIN MAKES THE GRASS MANY SHADES GREENER...

SO OUR PROSPECTS BRIGHTEN ON THE INFLUX OF BETTER THOUGHTS...

FAR OFF AS I LIVED, I WAS NOT EXEMPTED FROM THE ANNUAL VISITATION WHICH OCCURS, METHINKS, ABOUT THE FIRST OF APRIL, WHEN EVERYBODY IS ON THE MOVE...

GIRLS and BOYS and YOUNG WOMEN GENERALLY SEEMED TO BE GLAD TO BE IN THE WOODS...

THEY LOOKED IN THE POND and AT THE
FLOWERS and IMPROVED THEIR TIME...

BUT MEN OF BUSINESS, EVEN FARMERS, THOUGHT ONLY OF THE SOLITUDE and EMPLOYMENT—

??

and THE GREAT DISTANCE AT WHICH I DWELT FROM SOMETHING OR OTHER...

THEN THERE WERE DOCTORS, LAWYERS...

?? ??

TSK!

UNEASY HOUSEKEEPERS...

MINISTERS WHO SPOKE OF GOD AS IF THEY ENJOYED A MONO-POLY ON THE SUBJECT...

and YOUNG MEN WHO HAD CEASED TO BE YOUNG—

WHO HAD CONCLUDED THAT IT WAS SAFEST TO FOLLOW THE BEATEN PATH...

A MAN SITS AS MANY RISKS AS HE RUNS...

I HAD MY SHARE OF GOOD LUCK...

THOUGH THERE WERE SOME CURIOUS SPECIMENS AMONG MY VISITORS...

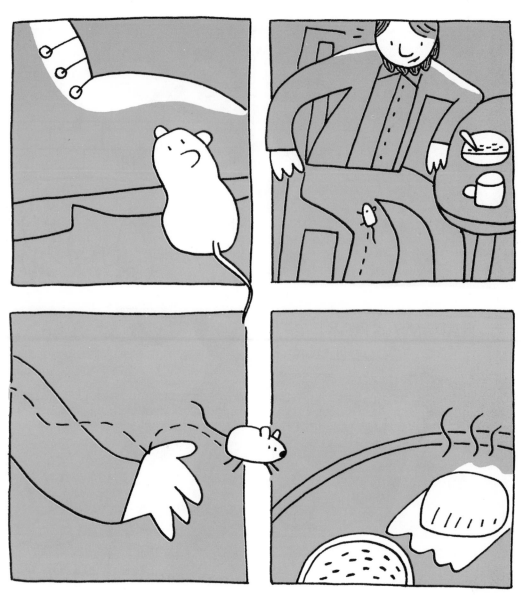

...MY GREATEST SKILL HAS BEEN TO WANT BUT LITTLE...

RATHER THAN LOVE, THAN MONEY, THAN FAME...

GIVE ME TRUTH...

GIVE ME THE POVERTY THAT ENJOYS TRUE WEALTH.

REGULARLY, AT HALF PAST SEVEN... AFTER THE EVENING TRAIN HAD GONE BY, THE WHIP-POOR-WILLS CHANTED THEIR VESPERS FOR HALF AN HOUR...

SITTING ON A STUMP BY MY DOOR, OR UPON THE RIDGE-POLE OF THE HOUSE...

WHIP-POOR-WILL

I HAD A RARE OPPORTUNITY TO BECOME FAMILIAR WITH THEIR HABITS...

THEY SANG AT INTERVALS THROUGHOUT THE NIGHT...

-POOR-WILL...

and WERE AGAIN AS MUSICAL AS EVER JUST BEFORE and ABOUT DAWN...

WHIP- POOR-WILL

I WAS ALSO SERENADED BY A HOOTING OWL...

Hoo hoo
hoo...
HOORER
Hoo...

I REJOICE THAT THERE ARE OWLS.

Hoo hoo
Hoo...
Hoo
Hoo...

Part Three

THE PHILOSOPHER'S STYLE OF LIVING IS ONLY OUTWARDLY SIMPLE, BUT INWARDLY COMPLEX...

WHAT DO WE WANT MOST TO DWELL NEAR TO...

...BUT THE PERENNIAL SOURCE OF OUR LIFE?

I HAD THIS ADVANTAGE, AT LEAST, IN MY MODE OF LIFE, OVER THOSE WHO WERE OBLIGED TO LOOK ABROAD FOR AMUSEMENT, TO SOCIETY and THE THEATRE...

THAT MY LIFE ITSELF WAS BECOME MY AMUSEMENT and NEVER CEASED TO BE NOVEL...

MANY A FORENOON HAVE I STOLEN AWAY, PREFERRING TO SPEND THUS THE MOST VALUED PART OF THE DAY, FOR I WAS RICH, IF NOT IN MONEY, IN SUNNY HOURS and SUMMER DAYS...

I AM NATURALLY NO HERMIT...

I THINK I LOVE SOCIETY AS MUCH AS MOST.

UNDER THE GROVE OF ELMS and BUTTONWOODS WAS A VILLAGE OF BUSY MEN...

I WENT THERE FREQUENTLY TO OBSERVE THEIR HABITS...

SNK!

I HAVE PAID NO POLL TAX FOR SIX YEARS...

ONE AFTERNOON... WHEN I WENT TO THE VILLAGE TO GET A SHOE FROM THE COBBLERS, I WAS SEIZED and PUT INTO JAIL...

BECAUSE I DID NOT PAY A TAX TO, OR RECOGNIZE THE AUTHORITY OF, THE STATE WHICH BUYS and SELLS MEN, WOMEN, and CHILDREN, LIKE CATTLE AT THE DOORS OF ITS SENATE-HOUSE...

THE NIGHT IN PRISON WAS NOVEL and INTERESTING ENOUGH...

THE PRISONERS IN THEIR SHIRTSLEEVES WERE ENJOYING A CHAT and THE EVENING AIR, WHEN I ENTERED...

BUT THE JAILER SAID "COME, BOYS, IT IS TIME TO LOCK UP."

MY ROOMMATE WAS INTRODUCED TO ME AS "A FIRST-RATE FELLOW and A CLEVER MAN."

KLANG-

WHEN THE DOOR WAS LOCKED HE SHOWED ME WHERE TO HANG MY HAT...

... I SAW THAT IF ONE STAYED THERE LONG, HIS PRINCIPAL BUSINESS WOULD BE TO LOOK OUT THE WINDOW...

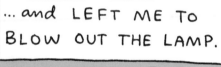
AT LENGTH HE SHOWED ME WHICH WAS MY BED

... and LEFT ME TO BLOW OUT THE LAMP.

NO MAN EVER FOLLOWED HIS GENIUS TILL IT MISLED HIM...

GOODNESS IS THE ONLY INVESTMENT THAT NEVER FAILS...

IN THE MORNING... WHEN I CAME OUT
OF PRISON — FOR SOME ONE HAD
INTERFERED, and PAID THAT TAX —
I DID NOT PERCEIVE THAT GREAT CHANGES
HAD TAKEN PLACE ON THE COMMON...
and YET A CHANGE HAD TO MY EYES
COME OVER THE SCENE... I SAW YET
MORE DISTINCTLY THE STATE IN WHICH
I LIVED...

I SAW TO WHAT EXTENT THE PEOPLE AMONG WHOM I LIVED COULD BE TRUSTED AS GOOD NEIGHBORS and FRIENDS;

THAT THEIR FRIENDSHIP WAS FOR SUMMER WEATHER ONLY...

THAT THEY HOPED, BY A CERTAIN OUTWARD OBSERVANCE, and A FEW PRAYERS, and BY WALKING IN A PARTICULAR STRAIGHT THOUGH USELESS PATH FROM TIME TO TIME, TO SAVE THEIR SOULS...

...THEY DO NOT KNOW BY HOW MUCH TRUTH IS STRONGER THAN ERROR...

I PROCEEDED TO FINISH MY ERRAND...

COBBLER

and, HAVING PUT ON MY MENDED SHOE—

...JOINED A HUCKLEBERRY PARTY

and IN HALF AN HOUR... WAS IN THE MIDST OF A HUCKLEBERRY FIELD, ON ONE OF OUR HIGHEST HILLS...

...TWO MILES OFF...

and THEN THE STATE WAS NOWHERE TO BE SEEN.

Part Four

OCTOBER ANSWERS TO THAT PERIOD IN THE LIFE OF MAN WHEN HE IS NO LONGER DEPENDENT ON HIS TRANSIENT MOODS, WHEN ALL HIS EXPERIENCE RIPENS INTO WISDOM, BUT EVERY ROOT, BRANCH, LEAF OF HIM GLOWS WITH MATURITY...

WHAT HE HAS BEEN and DONE IN HIS SPRING and SUMMER APPEARS...

HE BEARS HIS FRUIT....

I GO and COME WITH A STRANGE LIBERTY IN NATURE...

...A PART OF HERSELF...

I AM NO MORE LONELY THAN A SINGLE MULLEIN OR DANDELION IN A PASTURE, OR A BEAN LEAF, OR SORREL, OR A HORSE-FLY, OR A HUMBLEBEE...

I AM NO MORE LONELY THAN THE MILL BROOK, OR A WEATHERCOCK, OR THE NORTH STAR, OR THE SOUTH WIND...

OR AN APRIL SHOWER, OR A JANUARY THAW

...OR THE FIRST SPIDER IN A NEW HOUSE.

MORNING IS WHEN I AM AWAKE and
THERE IS A NEW DAWN IN ME...

OUR VILLAGE LIFE WOULD STAGNATE IF IT WERE NOT FOR THE UNEXPLORED FORESTS and MEADOWS WHICH SURROUND IT...

AT THE SAME TIME THAT WE ARE EARNEST TO EXPLORE and LEARN all THINGS, WE REQUIRE THAT all THINGS BE MYSTERIOUS and UNEXPLAINABLE...

... THAT LAND and SEA BE INFINITELY WILD, UNSURVEYED and UNFATHOMED BY US BECAUSE UNFATHOMABLE...

WE CAN NEVER HAVE ENOUGH OF NATURE.

WE NEED TO WITNESS OUR OWN LIMITS
TRANSGRESSED, and SOME LIFE PASTURING
FREELY WHERE WE NEVER WANDER...

...IN WILDNESS IS THE PRESERVATION
OF THE WORLD.

I DO NOT KNOW WHAT MADE ME LEAVE THE POND. I LEFT IT AS UNACCOUNTABLY AS I WENT TO IT...

TO SPEAK SINCERELY, I WENT THERE BECAUSE I HAD GOT READY TO GO; I LEFT IT FOR THE SAME REASON.

IT IS REMARKABLE HOW EASILY and
INSENSIBLY WE FALL INTO A PARTICULAR
ROUTE, and MAKE A BEATEN TRACK FOR
OURSELVES...

HOW WORN and DUSTY, THEN, MUST BE
THE HIGHWAYS OF THE WORLD, HOW DEEP
THE RUTS OF TRADITION and CONFORMITY.

I WENT TO THE WOODS TO LIVE DELIBERATELY, TO FRONT ONLY THE ESSENTIAL FACTS OF LIFE, and SEE IF I COULD NOT LEARN WHAT IT HAD TO TEACH —

and NOT, WHEN I CAME TO DIE, DISCOVER THAT I HAD NOT LIVED.

I LEARNED THIS, AT LEAST, BY MY EXPERIMENTS; THAT IF ONE ADVANCES CONFIDENTLY IN THE DIRECTION OF HIS DREAMS, and ENDEAVORS TO LIVE THE LIFE WHICH HE HAS IMAGINED —

HE WILL MEET WITH A SUCCESS UNEXPECTED IN COMMON HOURS...

HEAVEN IS UNDER OUR FEET AS WELL AS OVER OUR HEADS.

Afterword

Thoreau at Walden is, like *Walden* itself, not a definitive or chronological account of Thoreau's stay at the pond, but rather an impression of his experience there, and the philosophy that both brought him to its shores and resulted from his time there.

Thoreau believed that though circumstances and times change, though people and even civilizations come and go, the human experience remains the same. The spirit that drove the ancient Greeks and Hindus, the medieval scholars, drove the men of his day as well.

Likewise, here in twenty-first-century America, more than 150 years after Thoreau's famous experiment at Walden Pond, his life and words are as resonant and meaningful as ever.

All the words in this book, with a few exceptions, come directly from Thoreau's published writings (though I've taken the liberty of altering punctuation when necessary, and combining and rearranging the quotations to make the story flow). With that in mind, an annotation follows, identifying each quotation and where it can be found in editions of Thoreau's work that are currently in print and easily available.

My hope is that interested readers will be encouraged to seek out and explore the life and work of this incredible thinker (and doer), and to find the inspiration then, in their own lives, to fiercely explore themselves and their world—to move through life with self-confidence, curiosity, and resolve—as did Henry David Thoreau.

John Porcellino
DENVER, COLORADO
MARCH 1, 2007

Thoreau at Walden
Panel Discussions

PAGE 1: Henry David Thoreau was born in the small town of Concord, Massachusetts, on July 12, 1817. He lived almost his entire life in the town, and as a child developed a deep love and respect for the woodlands and fields around it. Concord, during Thoreau's lifetime in the mid-nineteenth century, was a major center of progressive American thought and literature. Thoreau counted among his friends and townspeople such major figures as the philosopher and writer Ralph Waldo Emerson (who took on a kind of paternal relation to the younger Henry David), the poet William Ellery Channing, the writer Nathaniel Hawthorne (*The Scarlet Letter*), and Louisa May Alcott (author of *Little Women*).

Thoreau was a member of a group of thinkers known as the transcendentalists. Transcendentalism was a uniquely American philosophy that combined elements of English romanticism, German idealism, and shades of thought informed by Eastern religions, particularly Indian Hinduism (Thoreau was especially fond of the *Bhagavad Gita*).

Their philosophy emphasized the superiority of individual, personal intuition over religious dogma and social conformity. They believed in an inner truth that transcended the merely physical or mental, and that this truth was available to all people through direct, intuitive understanding.

Also prevalent at the time in Thoreau's New England were experiments with utopian artistic and spiritual communities, where members chose to live outside mainstream society in order to be better able to explore these transcendentalist ways of life. Inspired in part by these experiments—and their failures—Thoreau, in the mid 1840s, began searching for land on which he could live alone but in near proximity to town life, so that he could pursue his intellectual and literary interests with less distraction.

PAGE 2: Contemporary accounts describe Thoreau as always dressing very plainly, with scuffed boots, a straw hat, and drab corduroy clothes. He was known for his plainspoken, uncouth manners and actions. Mainstream members of Concord society considered him an oddball.

"Beware of all enterprises that require new clothes." (w22)

PAGE 12: In the spring of 1845, Thoreau began building his house on land near Walden Pond owned by Ralph Waldo Emerson, about a mile and a half from Concord. He took up residence there on July 4, 1845.

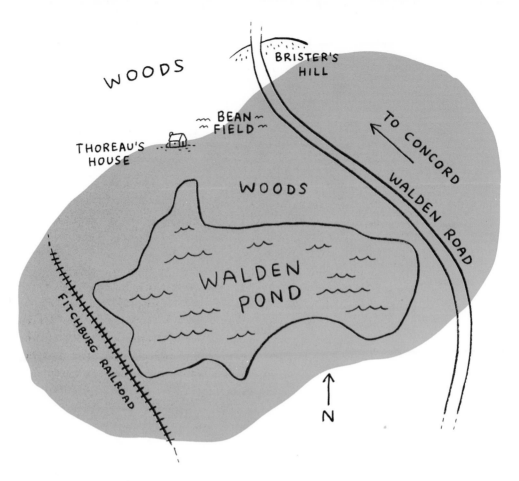

WOODS

BRISTER'S HILL

BEAN FIELD

THOREAU'S HOUSE

WOODS

TO CONCORD

WALDEN ROAD

FITCHBURG RAILROAD

WALDEN POND

N

"I have thus a tight shingled and plastered house, ten feet wide by fifteen feet long, and eight-feet posts with a garret and a closet, and a large window on each side, two trap doors, one door at the end, and a brick fireplace opposite." (w47)

"My nearest neighbor is a mile distant, and no house visible from any place but the hill-tops within half a mile of my own. I have my horizon bounded by woods all to myself; a distant view of the railroad where it touches the pond on the one hand, and of the fence which skirts the woodland road on the other." (w125)

"My house was on the side of a hill, on the edge of the larger wood, in the midst of a young forest of pitch-pines and hickories, and a half a

dozen rods* from the pond, to which a narrow footpath led down the hill. In my front yard grew the strawberry, blackberry and life-everlasting, johnswort and golden-rod, shrub oaks and sand-cherry, blueberry and ground-nut." (w110)

*A rod equals 16 ½ feet. Thoreau's house was actually about twelve rods from the shore.

PAGE 13: "… my three legged table from which I did not remove the books and pen and ink…" (w110)

Thoreau's furniture at Walden "consisted of a bed, a table, a desk, three chairs, a looking glass [mirror] three inches in diameter, a pair of tongs and andirons, a kettle, a skillet, and a frying pan, a dipper, a wash-bowl, two knives and forks, three plates, one cup, one spoon, a jug for oil, a jug for molasses and a japanned [lacquered] lamp." (w63)

PAGE 18: *"I long ago lost a hound..."*
The meaning of this famous, poetic passage has been argued for years, with no definitive scholarly answer, but these three animals are believed to be symbolic to Thoreau of some personal loss, or losses.

PAGES 20–22: *Owl Incident*
"One afternoon I amused myself by watching a barred owl (*Strix nebulosa*) sitting on one of the lower dead limbs of a white-pine, close to the trunk, in broad daylight, I standing within a rod of him. He could hear me when I moved and cronched the snow with my feet, but could not plainly see me. When I made most noise he would stretch out his neck and erect his neck feathers, and open his eyes wide; but their lids soon fell again, and he began to nod. I too felt a slumberous influence after watching him half an hour." (w257)

PAGE 30: "I got up early and bathed in the pond; that was a religious exercise and one of the best things which I did." (w86)

PAGE 36: *"I was determined to know beans."* (w156)
Thoreau planted beans and other crops for food, but also to sell, in order to "earn ten or twelve dollars by some honest and agreeable method." (w52) His first growing season at Walden he reckons: "I got twelve bushels of beans, and eighteen bushels of potatoes, beside some peas and sweet corn. The yellow corn and turnips were too late to come to any thing." (w53) He earned $23.44 from his harvest, and, deducting his costs of $14.72 ½, calculated a profit of $8.71 ½. (During his time at Walden, Thoreau also did odd jobs in town to earn some money: building fences, painting, gardening, and so forth.) Thoreau's goal was not to avoid conventional work but to live simply enough to be able to easily afford his chosen way of life. "...I found that by working about six weeks in a year I could meet all the expenses of living." (w66)

PAGE 47: Far from being totally isolated, Thoreau had many encounters with his townsfolk in the woods, both curious parties who came to see him, and friends, as well as the children of his friends, who enjoyed playing near the pond with him. "Many a traveler came out of his way to see me and the inside of my house..." (w145)

PAGE 51: *Food*
Thoreau's food at Walden was very simple: "[bread made from] rye and Indian [corn] meal without yeast, potatoes, rice, a very little salt pork, molasses, and salt; and my drink, water." (w58) Visitors also report meals of roasted fish, corn, and beans. That said, he made frequent trips into town where he'd often enjoy more traditional meals at home, or with his friends.

"...men have come to such a pass that they frequently starve, not for want of necessities, but from want of luxuries." (w59)

PAGE 52: *Mouse Incident*
"The mice which haunted my house were not the common ones, which are said to be introduced into the country, but a wild

native kind not found in the village...When I was building, one of these [mice] had its nest underneath the house, and before I had laid the second floor, and swept out the shavings, would come out regularly at lunch time and pick up the crumbs at my feet. It probably had never seen a man before; and it soon became quite familiar, and would run over my shoes and up my clothes. It could readily ascend the sides of the room by short impulses, like a squirrel, which it resembled in its motions. At length, as I leaned with my elbow on the bench one day, it ran up my clothes and along my sleeve, and round and round the paper which held my dinner, while I kept the latter close, and dodged and played at bo-peep* with it; and when at last I held still a piece of cheese between my thumb and finger, it came and nibbled it, sitting in my hand, and afterward cleaned its face and paws, like a fly, and walked away." (w216–17)

* "peek-a-boo"

PAGE 62: Although he sought a simple existence on the edges of society, Thoreau maintained his connections to town life, visiting Concord frequently to do errands, to see family and friends, and to work at the occasional odd job. Thoreau sought not to *escape* society, but to improve it.

"The Fitchburg Railroad touches the pond about a hundred rods from where I dwell. I usually go to the village along its causeway..." (w112)

PAGE 63: *"I have paid no poll tax..."*

A poll tax is a fixed tax levied by state or local governments on a per person basis. Each member of the community paid a set rate every year (in Concord, at the time, the tax was about $1.50 per year).

Thoreau, like many (if not all) transcenden-

talists, was an abolitionist, dedicated to ending the institution of slavery in America. He refused to pay the tax in protest over Massachusetts's complicity in American slavery (though Massachusetts was a free state, its textile industries depended on cotton grown using slave labor in the South). Additionally, Thoreau's refusal to pay was in protest of the Mexican-American War, then being fought over the annexation of Texas and other Mexican territories by the United States. Abolitionists feared that the newly annexed territories would create more slave-holding U.S. states.

PAGE 64: One day in late July 1846, when Thoreau was in town running errands, he was stopped by the local tax collector, Sam Staples, who requested payment of Thoreau's delinquent taxes. Thoreau refused (Staples then offered to pay Thoreau's tax himself, which Thoreau also refused) and so was taken to the county jail.

That night, an embarrassed relative, most likely his aunt Maria Thoreau, paid Henry's delinquent tax for him, and he was released the next morning.

PAGE 72: "...one of our highest hills..." refers to Fair Haven Hill, located half a mile from Walden Pond, which was a beloved local haunt of Thoreau's.

PAGE 77: "Every man looks at his wood-pile with a kind of affection." (w241)

PAGE 80: *Environmentalism.*

As he grew older, Thoreau became more and more interested in studying, documenting, and scientifically understanding the world around him. He struck up a correspondence with the European naturalist Louis Agassiz, and made detailed studies of the plants and animals he found on his walks throughout the Concord countryside.

Some critics have complained that the lofty, philosophical musings of Thoreau's earlier writings later gave way to drier, more academic works of natural history, and he has been accused of scientific amateurism; but in fact his later works anticipate aspects of modern ecological thought, and some of these writings, like "The Succession of Forest Trees," are acknowledged now as having made important headway in our understanding of natural systems. Today, Thoreau is considered by many to be a forefather of the modern environmentalist movement.

PAGE 85: *Leaving Walden*
In the late summer of 1847, Thoreau's friend

Emerson was leaving for an extended European lecture tour, and Thoreau was invited to stay in Emerson's home in town while he was away. On September 6, 1847, Thoreau left his house at Walden Pond, two years, two months and two days after he had arrived. During his stay at Walden, he wrote two drafts of his first book *A Week on the Concord and Merrimack Rivers*, the essays "Ktaadn" and "Resistance to Civil Government" (later edited into "Civil Disobedience"), and an early version of *Walden*.

Walden, first published in 1849, was met with little reaction from readers and critics at the time, but has since come to be acknowledged as one of the greatest works of nineteenth-century American writing, indeed one of the great works of world literature.

Henry David Thoreau passed away on May 6, 1862, at his family home in Concord. He was forty-four years old.

....

Quotation Sources

Key to Sources: Each quotation from the book is listed by page, and is followed by a guide code to help the reader locate the phrase in its original context.

CD: "Civil Disobedience," as found in *The Essays of Henry D. Thoreau*, edited by Lewis Hyde.
J: from Thoreau's lifelong handwritten journal, with date.
W: *Walden, a Fully Annotated Edition*, edited by Jeffrey S. Cramer.
WK: "Walking," as found in *The Essays of Henry D. Thoreau*, edited by Lewis Hyde.

Example: "W121" is found on page 121 of *Walden: a Fully Annotated Edition*.

PROLOGUE
P. 2: "The mass of men ... desperation" W7
P. 2: "I see young ... rid of" W3
P. 3: "Why should ... born" W3
P. 3: "It is very ... limits" W5
P. 3: "Trying to ... debt" W6
P. 4: "Making yourselves ... day" W6
P. 4: "But men labor ... mistake" W3
P. 4: "They honestly ... left" W7
P. 5: "It would be ... obtain them" W11

P. 5: "Shall we ... with less" W35
P. 6: "The greater ... behavior" W10
P. 6: "I hear ... voice" W10
P. 7: "which invites ... that" W10

PART ONE
P. 12: "I lived alone ... Massachusetts" W1
P. 13: "And earned ... hands only" W1
P. 14: "To be a philosopher ... trust" W14
P. 15: "It is to solve ... practically" W14

Bibliography

Lawrence, Jerome and Lee, Robert E. *The Night Thoreau Spent in Jail: A Play*. New York: Hill and Wang, 1971 (2001 edition).

Maynard, W. Barksdale. *Walden Pond: A History*. New York: Oxford University Press, 2004.

Richardson Jr., Robert D. *Henry Thoreau: A Life of the Mind*. Berkeley and Los Angeles: California University Press, 1986.

Thoreau, Henry David. *The Essays of Henry D. Thoreau*. Selected and edited by Lewis Hyde. New York: North Point Press, 2002.

Thoreau, Henry David. *Walden: A Fully Annotated Edition*. Edited and annotated by Jeffrey S. Cramer. New Haven, CT and London: Yale University Press, 2004.

Credits

INTRODUCTION

D. B. JOHNSON has been a freelance illustrator for more than twenty years, contributing editorial cartoons, comic strips, and conceptual illustrations to magazines and newspapers around the country. Mr. Johnson's first picture book, *Henry Hikes to Fitchburg*, based on the life of Henry David Thoreau, was a *New York Times* and *Publishers Weekly* bestseller. *Henry Hikes to Fitchburg* also won numerous awards, including the Boston Globe–Horn Book Award for Picture Books. D. B. lives in an "urban cabin" with his wife in New Hampshire.

WRITER/ARTIST

JOHN PORCELLINO has been writing, drawing, and publishing minicomics, comics, and graphic novels for the last twenty-five years. His celebrated series King-Cat Comics, begun in 1989, has inspired a generation of cartoonists. *Diary of a Mosquito Abatement Man*, a collection of *King-Cat* stories about Porcellino's experiences as a pest control worker, won an Ignatz Award in 2005. *Perfect Example*, first published in 2000, chronicles his struggles with depression as a teenager. According to cartoonist Chris Ware, "John Porcellino's comics distill, in just a few lines and words, the feeling of simply being alive." Porcellino lives in Denver with his wife, Misun, and a small black cat named Maisie Kukoc. Visit www.king-cat.net

SERIES EDITOR

JAMES STURM is the cofounder and director of The Center for Cartoon Studies. His most recent graphic novel is *James Sturm's America*. James's writings and illustrations have appeared in the pages of *The Chronicles of Higher Education*, *The Onion*, *The New York Times*, and on the cover of *The New Yorker*.